MADGE'S MAGIC SHOW

MADGE'S MAGIC SHOW

by Mike Thaler

illustrated by
Carol Nicklaus

An Easy-Read Story Book
Franklin Watts
New York/London/1978

For Kathleen Kennedy
to teach with love

26733

Library of Congress Cataloging in Publication Data

Thaler, Mike, 1936-
  Madge's magic show.

  (An Easy-read story book)
  SUMMARY: Madge is a great magician and
easily pulls several animals out of her hat — but
not the one she wants.
  [1. Magicians—Fiction] I. Nicklaus, Carol. II. Title.
PZ7.T3Mad   [E]   77-17288
ISBN 0-531-01450-9 lib. bdg.
ISBN 0-531-02232-3

R.L. 2.2 Spache Revised Formula
Text copyright © 1978 by Michael C. Thaler
Illustrations copyright © 1978 by Carol Nicklaus
Printed in the United States of America
6 5 4 3 2 1

MADGE'S MAGIC SHOW

Madge was very special.
She was a great magician.

She had a hat, a cape,
and a wand.

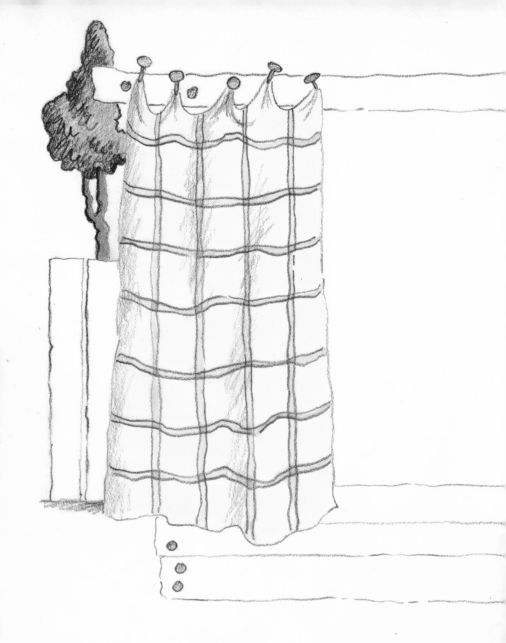

She even had

a stage.

One day she decided to give
a magic show.
Everyone came from miles around

...except Jimmy Smith.

He just leaned over the fence.

Madge waved her wand.

"Abracadabra. Moons and Stars.

Blinkies and Twinkies, hello!

Get set to see some magic.

I'm Madge the Magnifico!"

Everyone smiled...
except Jimmy Smith.
He yawned.

"This is my first trick," Madge said.
"I will turn this water...orange."
And she did.
Everyone cheered.

"That's not so hard,"
said Jimmy Smith.

Madge looked over the fence.
She wiggled her ears, and turned
her back.

"I will now pull six
scarves from this empty box."
And she did.

Everyone clapped.
"Scarves are dumb,"
said Jimmy Smith.

Madge stuck out her chin.
She threw back her cape,
and took off her hat.

"And now if you'll be quiet," she said.
"I will do my finest trick—
never before seen on Chestnut Street.
I will pull one fluffy, baby rabbit
out of this very hat!"

"You can't pull a rabbit out
of that hat," said Jimmy Smith.
Madge said her magic words.
She reached into her hat, and
pulled out...

a chicken!

"Gee, that's terrific," said Freddy Jones.

"A chicken is not a rabbit,"
said Jimmy Smith.

"Give me a little time," said Madge.
She reached back into her hat.
She said the magic words, and
pulled out...

a turkey!

"Ha!" said Jimmy Smith.

"That's not a rabbit either."

Madge's face turned red.

She waved her hand.

She reached in, and pulled out...

a goat!

The goat began to eat Madge's cape.

Everybody laughed.

"I knew she couldn't do it!"

said Jimmy Smith.

"One more time," Madge said.
She reached slowly into her hat.
She said the magic words, and
pulled out...

a horse!

"Wow! A real horse," said all the kids.
"I told you she couldn't do it,"
said Jimmy Smith.

Madge put on her hat.

"I guess the show is over," she said.

She tied on what was left of

her cape.

Just then the hat began to move.
A little pink nose stuck out
from under the brim.
"A rabbit!" said Madge.
"What took you so long?"

The little rabbit hopped to the ground.

Everyone clapped and cheered.

"Gee," said Jimmy Smith.

"A real rabbit. How did you do it?"

"It was nothing," said Madge,
tapping her hat.
"All us great magicians know how."